■ Science Experiments for Young People ■

Environmental Experiments

About

AIR

Thomas R. Rybolt

and

Robert C. Mebane

ENSLOW PUBLISHERS, INC.

Bloy St. and Ramsey Ave.	P.O. Box 38
Box 777	Aldershot
Hillside, N.J. 07205	Hants GU12 6BP
U.S.A.	U.K.

For my daughter, Leah, with love — TR

For Harden, Sharon, and Chelsea. — RM

Library of Congress Cataloging-in-Publication Data

Rybolt, Thomas R.
    Environmental experiments about air/Thomas R. Rybolt and Robert C. Mebane.
        p. cm. — (Science experiments for young people)
    Includes index.
    Summary: Uses text and experiments to provide information about
the air around us and about pollution and other problems related to
our atmosphere.
    ISBN 0-89490-409-4
        1. Air—Pollution—Experiments—Juvenile literature.
2. Greenhouse effect, Atmospheric—Experiments—Juvenile literature.
3. Air—Experiments—Juvenile literature. [1.Air—Experiments.
2. Air—Pollution—Experiments. 3. Greenhouse effect, Atmospheric—
Experiments. 4. Experiments.] I. Mebane, Robert C. II. Title.
III. Series.
TD883.13.R93 1993
628.5′3′078—dc20   92-26297
                                    CIP
                                      AC

Printed in the United States of America

10 9 8 7 6 5 4 3 2

Illustration Credit: Kimberly Austin

Cover Illustration: © John Shaw/Tom Stack & Associates

CONTENTS

series contents for
SCIENCE EXPERIMENTS
FOR YOUNG PEOPLE

Introduction

Earth

Earth, our home in space, has supported life for billions of years. But with a growing human population, people are having a greater effect on the environment than ever before. Together we must learn about the problems facing our environment and work to protect the earth.

There are many ways we can work together to protect the earth. We can ask adults to use more fuel-efficient cars (cars that get more miles per gallon of gasoline). We can ride bikes or walk instead of getting rides in cars. We can recycle aluminum, paper, plastic, and glass, and we can plant trees. We can save energy by turning off lights when they are not in use. We can save energy by not keeping rooms and buildings too hot in the winter or too cold in the summer. Another way we can help the earth is to learn more about the environment.

This series of environmental books is designed to help you better understand our environment by doing experiments with air, water, land, and life. Each book is divided into chapters on topics of environmental concern or importance. There is a brief introduction to each chapter followed by a group of experiments related to the chapter topic. This series of environmental experiment books is intended to be used and not just read. It is your guide to doing, observing, and thinking about your environment.

By understanding our environment, we can learn to protect the earth and to use our natural resources wisely for generations to come.

Atoms and Molecules

Understanding something about atoms and molecules will help you understand our environment. Everything in the world around us is made of atoms and molecules. Atoms are the basic building blocks of all things. There are about 100 different kinds of atoms. Molecules are combinations of tightly bound atoms. For example, a water molecule is a combination of two hydrogen atoms and one oxygen atom.

Molecules that are made of only a few atoms are very small. Just one drop of water contains about two million quadrillion (2,000,000,000,000,000,000,000,000) water molecules.

Polymers are large molecules that may contain millions of atoms. Important natural polymers include natural rubber, starch, and DNA. Some important artificial polymers are nylon, which is used in making fabrics, polyethylene, which is used to make plastic bags and plastic bottles, and polystyrene, which is used in making styrofoam cups and insulation.

Atoms are made of smaller particles called electrons, protons, and neutrons. The nucleus is the center of the atom and contains protons and neutrons. Protons are positively charged, and neutrons have no charge. Electrons are negatively charged and surround the nucleus and give the atom its size.

Atoms and molecules that are charged are called ions. Ions have either a positive charge or a negative charge. Positive ions have more protons than electrons. Negative ions have more electrons than protons. Sodium chloride, which is the chemical name for table salt, is made of positive sodium ions and negative chlorine ions.

Atoms, ions, and molecules can combine in chemical reactions to make new substances. Chemical reactions can change one substance into another or break one substance down into smaller parts made of molecules, atoms, or ions.

Science and Experiments

One way to learn more about the environment and science is to do experiments. Science experiments provide a way of asking questions and finding answers. The results that come from experiments and observations increase our knowledge and improve our understanding of the world around us.

Science will never have all the answers because there are always experiments that you can do at home or at school. As you read about science and do experiments, you will learn more about our planet and its environment.

Not every experiment you do will work the way you expect every time. Something may be different in the experiment when you do it. Repeat the experiment if it gives an unexpected result and think about what may be different.

Not all of the experiments in this book give immediate results. Some experiments in this book will take time to see observable results. Some of the experiments in this book may take a shorter time than that suggested in the experiment. Some experiments may take a longer time than suggested.

Each experiment is divided into five parts: (1) materials, (2) procedure, (3) observations, (4) discussion, and (5) other things to try. The materials are what you need to do the experiment. The procedure is what you do. The observations are what you see. The discussion explains what your observations tell you about the environment. The other things to try are additional questions and experiments.

Safety Note

Make Sure You:

- Obtain an adult's permission before you do these experiments and activities.
- Get an adult to watch you when you do an experiment. They enjoy seeing experiments too.
- Follow the specific directions given for each experiment.
- Clean up after each experiment.

Note to Teachers, Parents, and Other Adults

Science is not merely a collection of facts but a way of thinking. As a teacher, parent, or adult friend, you can play a key role in maintaining and encouraging a young person's interest in science and the surrounding world. As you do environmental experiments with a young person, you may find your own curiosity being expanded. Experiments are one way to learn more about the air, water, land, and life upon which we all depend.

I. Oxygen and Carbon Dioxide

The earth is surrounded by an invisible blanket of air called the atmosphere. Just as the ocean is filled with water, the atmosphere is filled with air. Without air, there could be no life on earth.

Air is a mixture of different gases. Dry air consists mostly of nitrogen, oxygen, argon, and carbon dioxide. We know that out of every 10,000 molecules in dry air there are approximately 7,810 nitrogen molecules, 2,094 oxygen molecules, 93 argon molecules, and 3 carbon dioxide molecules. Other gases in the air are present in even smaller amounts. Air may also contain molecules of water. Humid or wet air may contain as many as 400 water molecules out of every 10,000 molecules in air.

Like other animals, humans must have oxygen to live. The food we eat is combined with oxygen from the air to produce the energy we need to live and extra carbon dioxide. With every breath, you inhale some oxygen and exhale some extra carbon dioxide.

The carbon dioxide produced by animals is used by plants. Plants use the energy from sunlight to combine nutrients, water, and carbon dioxide to produce sugar and other molecules. During this process, called photosynthesis, plants release oxygen, which can then be used by animals.

As you can see, plants and animals depend on each other for life. Animals produce carbon dioxide needed by plants, and plants produce oxygen needed by animals. Oxygen and carbon dioxide are the gases in the air that link all plants and animals together. It is essential that the proper balance of oxygen and carbon dioxide is maintained. In the following experiments you will learn more about oxygen and carbon dioxide.

How Much Oxygen Is in the Air?

Materials

Water	Clean steel wool
A tall, narrow jar	A piece of tape
A large cake pan	Vinegar

Procedure

Fill the pan almost full of water. Put the pan in a place where it can sit for several days without being moved.

Push a loose wad of clean steel wool into the bottom of a tall, narrow jar. The steel wool should stay in place when the jar is turned upside down. Pour enough vinegar into the jar to cover the steel wool completely. Wait about five minutes and then pour out the vinegar.

Completely fill the jar containing the steel wool with water. Cover the mouth of the jar with your hand and turn the jar upside down in the pan of water. Put your hand and the mouth of the jar under water. Remove your hand, but keep the mouth of the jar under water. The water will remain in the jar.

Now tilt the edge of the jar enough to let out some water. As water goes out of the jar, air goes in the jar. Let out enough water to bring the level in the jar down to just above the level of the water in the pan. Place the mouth of the jar on the bottom of the pan of water.

Put a piece of tape on the side of the jar to mark the level of the water inside the jar. Do not move the jar. Check the level of the water the next day.

Observations

Does the water level rise inside the jar? How much of the airfilled space in the jar has been filled with water?

Discussion

Steel wool is made of long thin pieces of steel, which is mostly iron. The iron in the steel combines with oxygen molecules in the air to form iron oxide and rust. Rust is a combination of water and iron oxide. Rust and iron oxide are solids. Rinsing the steel wool with vinegar speeds up the reaction.

The level of water in the jar should rise as oxygen molecules combine with iron atoms to form rust. About one-fifth of the air around us is made of oxygen molecules. At most, only about one-fifth of the air in your jar will be used up. Most of the rest of the air is nitrogen. The nitrogen molecules in the air do not combine with the iron atoms.

Other Things to Try

ASK AN ADULT TO HELP YOU WITH THIS EXPERIMENT. DO NOT USE MATCHES BY YOURSELF. Push a handful of playdough or modeling clay against the bottom of a cake pan. Push a small candle into the playdough. Fill the pan with water, but do not cover the top of the candle with water. Light the candle with a match and put a jar over the top of the candle. Watch the candle. Does the candle burn out after a short time?

The water level should rise some in the jar but may not rise as much as with the rusting steel wool. The burning candle uses up some of the oxygen gas in the jar and makes carbon dioxide gas. The candle will not burn when the oxygen level gets too low. Some of the heated air may expand and escape from the jar, which could also cause the water level to rise.

In a burning flame, carbon is combined with oxygen to produce carbon dioxide. Animals use oxygen and combine it with carbon from food to produce carbon dioxide. Humans like other animals could not live without oxygen.

Repeat the original experiment with a wad of fresh steel wool, but do not let the steel wool get wet. Is less oxygen used up? Does less rust form? When a metal gets wet, the metal tends to form rust more rapidly.

Do you know why the nitrogen molecules are not used up in these experiments? Nitrogen atoms in a nitrogen gas molecule are held so tightly together that they do not break apart as easily as oxygen. Usually, nitrogen in the air does not combine with other atoms. However, in lightning storms, sometimes nitrogen and oxygen molecules in the air are combined to make nitrogen oxide. The bolts of lightning have enough electrical and heat energy to cause nitrogen to react. Nitrogen oxide is a pollution molecule that is also produced in small amounts by automobiles.

Experiment #2

Does Your Breath Contain Carbon Dioxide?

Materials

Large jar with lid   Measuring cup

Small jar with lid   Water

Measuring spoon

Lime powder (use pickling lime available in grocery stores)

Procedure

DO NOT TASTE THE LIME POWDER OR LIME-WATER. DO NOT GET THE LIME POWDER OR LIME-WATER ON YOUR SKIN OR IN YOUR EYES OR IN YOUR MOUTH.

Pour two cups of water into a large jar and add one-half teaspoon of lime powder to the water. Tighten the lid on the jar and shake the jar for one minute. Set the jar down with the lid still on the jar. Wait about three hours for the undissolved lime to settle to the bottom of the jar. Open the jar and carefully pour the limewater into a small jar until it is half full. Do not pour any of the solid out of the large jar. Put the lid back on the large jar and save for further tests.

Tighten the lid on the small jar and shake for about twenty seconds. Observe the limewater. Now open the jar and blow into the jar about six times. DO NOT PUT YOUR MOUTH ON THE JAR. Now, quickly put the lid on the jar and shake the jar for about twenty seconds again.

Observations

How does the limewater in the small jar look before you blow into the jar? After you blow into the jar and shake the limewater, does it change color? Does it look different?

Discussion

The pickling lime you use in this experiment is a solid called calcium hydroxide, which will dissolve in water. Not all the lime dissolves in water. The white solid that settles to the bottom of the jar is undissolved lime.

The limewater contains ions of calcium that can combine with carbon dioxide dissolved in water to form calcium carbonate. Calcium carbonate, which is not very soluble in water, is the solid that gives the water a cloudy color.

Limewater can be used to test for carbon dioxide. Carbon dioxide turns limewater to a milky white or cloudy color. Although air contains carbon dioxide, it does not have enough of this gas to immediately change the limewater to a cloudy color. When you blow into the jar, you are blowing extra carbon dioxide into the jar.

This experiment shows you how you can test for carbon dioxide gas. Your breath does contain carbon dioxide gas. Humans like other animals breathe in air, remove some of the oxygen from air, and blow out air with extra carbon dioxide. Animals use oxygen and produce carbon dioxide. Plants use carbon dioxide and release oxygen into the air.

Other Things to Try

You can use this experiment to test the bubbles from a carbonated beverage for carbon dioxide. You can also test the gas made by mixing one half cup of vinegar and one teaspoon of baking soda. Tilt a carbonated beverage or jar with the vinegar and baking soda mixture to pour some of the gas into limewater.

You can test also for carbon dioxide in the air. Leave a jar of limewater open for several days and see if a thin layer of white calcium carbonate forms on the surface. When you shake the jar the limewater should turn cloudy. There is not as much carbon dioxide in the air as in your breath so it takes longer to see the same effect.

ASK AN ADULT TO HELP YOU WITH THIS EXPERIMENT. DO NOT USE MATCHES BY YOURSELF. Have an adult use a pair of tongs or pliers to hold a burning match in a jar containing clear limewater. After the match has burned, close the jar and shake for twenty seconds. Does the limewater turn cloudy? Do you expect burning wood to release carbon dioxide gas?

The process of forming calcium carbonate in the water removes carbon dioxide from the air. Do you see how marine animals that make shells out of calcium carbonate could help remove extra carbon dioxide from the air?

II. Our Protective Atmosphere

Our atmosphere is important to life in many ways. Besides holding gases needed by plants and animals to live, the atmosphere also is active in protecting life on earth.

The atmosphere is divided into different layers called the troposphere, stratosphere, and ionosphere. The ionosphere includes layers called the mesosphere and thermosphere. Each layer plays a different role in protecting life on earth.

The troposphere is the layer of air nearest to the earth. Weather, such as wind and rain, occurs in the troposphere. Wind and rising air help remove pollution from roadways, cities, and factories. Rain helps wash pollution out of the atmosphere. In addition, the molecules of water in the air keep excess heat from leaving the earth and going out into space. This greenhouse effect keeps the surface of the earth from being too cold for life.

The stratosphere, which is above the troposphere, contains a layer of gas called ozone. Ozone is a special type of oxygen molecule. Ozone in the upper atmosphere protects plants and animals from excessive, damaging ultraviolet radiation from the sun. In recent years, there has been a decrease in amount of ozone over part of the earth. This place in the ozone layer is called an ozone hole.

The ionosphere contains charged atoms and molecules that protect us from cosmic rays and harmful radiation given off by the sun.

It is important for us to understand our atmosphere and how it helps protect life on the earth. This knowledge will help us repair and prevent problems that could damage our atmosphere. In the following experiments, you will learn more about our atmosphere.

Experiment #3
How Can You Show the Presence of the Ionosphere Above the Earth?

Materials

An AM radio

Procedure

After the sun has gone down at night, turn on an AM radio. Tune the radio to find out what different stations you can receive. Listen to different stations until you find one that is coming from a distant city. Don't select a local station coming from a nearby city, but select one that is as far away as possible. You may want to look on a map or ask an adult about how far away the city is located.

Turn the radio off, but do not change the station. The next day before the sun goes down, turn on the radio. Don't change the station, but listen. Turn off the radio, and wait until nighttime. Turn on the radio again.

Observations

Could you hear the station clearly during the first night? Could you hear the station clearly the next day? Could you hear the station clearly the second night?

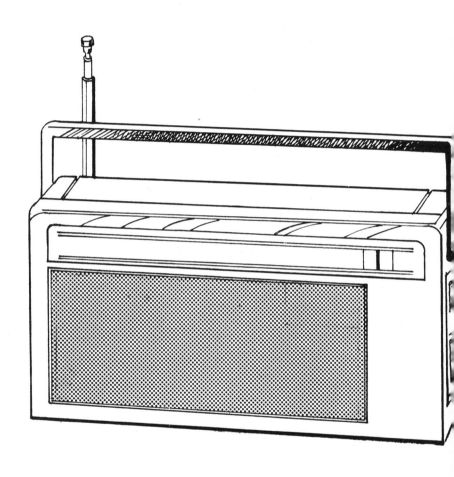

Discussion

You will usually find that you can pick up more distant AM (AM stands for amplitude modulation) radio stations at night than you can during the day. The radio station that was clear the first night could probably not be heard at all during the next day but was clear again the second night. If you did not make this observation, try again with a different radio station.

What is changing in the atmosphere to make distant radio stations clear at night but not clear during the day? You are detecting changes in the earth's ionosphere with your radio.

Charged atoms called ions in the ionosphere cause radio waves to be reflected back toward the earth. Radio waves bounce back and forth between the earth and the ionosphere. The difference in the position of the sun during the day and during the night causes changes in the ability of the ionosphere to reflect radio waves. Different layers of the ionosphere reflect different wavelengths or types of radio waves.

Radio waves are longer than television waves. The shorter TV waves pass right through the ionosphere. Television signals are sent long distances by satellite or by cable. However, with no special equipment, you can receive radio waves from radio stations that are hundreds of miles away.

The ionosphere is important because it helps protect us from cosmic rays and atomic particles emitted from the sun. The ionosphere is like a blanket of charged atoms that surrounds and protects life on earth from damaging radiation found in space.

The earth is surrounded by different layers of protecting atmosphere. The troposphere is the body of air up to about 10 miles (16 kilometers) above the earth. Most of the water vapor, dust, and air is located in the troposphere. The troposphere is responsible for the earth's weather. From 10 to 30 miles (50 kilometers) above the earth is the stratosphere. The stratosphere contains the thinner air and a layer of ozone that protects us from ultraviolet radiation.

Above the stratosphere, from 30 to 300 miles (500 kilometers) above the earth, is the ionosphere. The region where the ionosphere is found is also called the mesosphere (30 to 50 miles or 80 kilometers) and the thermosphere (50 to 600 miles or 965 kilometers). Beyond the thermosphere is outer space. In the ionosphere the very thin air is changed to ions because rays from the sun and cosmic rays from space knock electrons off of atoms and molecules leaving them with a positive charge.

In northern regions of the earth, colored lights in the sky called the aurora borealis are caused by atomic particles or solar radiation striking the ionosphere. At night, without the sun, the charged ions lose their charge, and the extra energy is given off as auroral light. This glow tends to follow the magnetic field of the earth and is concentrated near the poles. In southern regions toward the south pole, these colored lights are called the aurora australis. These beautiful displays of light remind us of the protection given to us by the earth's ionosphere.

Other Things to Try

See how many different radio stations you can pick up during the day. Mark where they are located on a map. You may have to listen to each station for a while until they tell in what city they are located.

See how many different radio stations you can pick up during the night. Mark where they are located on a map. Compare the daytime cities and nighttime cities. Are they different in how far away they are located?

You could try this experiment at different times during the year. Day and night AM radio reception may be much different in winter and summer.

Experiment #4

Do Differences in Temperature Cause Wind?

Materials

Pinwheel   Refrigerator freezer

Procedure

Hold the handle of the pinwheel so that the pinwheel is facing upward just beneath the refrigerator freezer compartment. Hold the pinwheel steady and slowly open the freezer door. After about thirty seconds, slowly move the pinwheel away from the front of the freezer compartment. Close the freezer door.

DO NOT LEAVE THE FREEZER OPEN FOR MORE THAN ABOUT A MINUTE AT A TIME.

Observations

Does the pinwheel begin to spin when you open the freezer door? Does the pinwheel stop spinning when you move it away from the freezer compartment?

Discussion

Warmer air is lighter or less dense than colder air because the molecules in warm air are farther apart from

each other. Lighter, less dense, hot air rises. Heavier, more dense, cooler air falls. As hot air rises, cooler air moves in to take its place, and wind is formed. Differences in temperature cause wind to flow.

When you open the freezer compartment, you should see the pinwheel begin to turn. The pinwheel continues to spin because cold air is falling past it, creating wind. The pinwheel should stop spinning when you move it away from the freezer compartment because there is no more falling air going past the pinwheel.

Wind helps carry pollution molecules away from the cities or factories where they may be produced. Pollution molecules build up in the air near where they are formed if there is no wind to carry them away or rain to wash them out of the air.

On the earth, it is coldest at the north and south poles and warmest at the equator. This difference in global temperatures causes our global patterns of wind flow. In general, warm air rises at the equator and travels toward the poles where the air is cooled and falls. The specific wind patterns are much more complicated because the earth is also spinning around every twenty-four hours as it travels through space.

The spinning earth and rising and falling of warm and cool air cause complicated global wind patterns. Near the equator there is little wind, and this region is called the doldrums. North and south of the equator is the region called the east trade winds. The next wind patterns are the horse latitudes, then the prevailing westerlies. Finally, in the polar regions, are the polar easterlies.

Other Things to Try

Blow on a pinwheel. Does it spin faster as you blow harder? Take the pinwheel outside on a windy day. Can you use the speed that the pinwheel turns to measure how fast the wind is blowing?

Hold the pinwheel facing down inside a lamp shade above a light bulb. DO NOT TOUCH THE LIGHT BULB OR ALLOW THE PINWHEEL TO TOUCH THE LIGHT BULB. When the light bulb is turned on, it gets quite warm. You may be able to use the pinwheel to measure the hot air rising above the bulb.

In addition to global wind flow, there are local winds. One of the causes of local wind patterns is the difference between high and low pressure fronts that move across the surface of the earth. Open a new bottle of a soft drink or carbonated beverage. Listen carefully. Do you hear the sound of moving air? A soft drink is in a pressurized bottle so that the pressure inside is greater than outside. A wind is caused because the air moves from the higher pressure to the lower pressure.

Along the land near the edge of the ocean, there is usually a constant sea breeze during the day. During the day, the land gets hotter than the water. The air above the hot land rises, and cooler, heavier air above the ocean moves in to take its place. This causes the sea breeze along many coasts or shorelines.

At night the air above the water is warmer than above the land, and the breeze flows from land to sea. This is called a land breeze.

You can demonstrate the difference in warming of land and water by this experiment. Fill one plastic cup with water. Fill another plastic cup with sand. On a hot, sunny day put both cups in the sunshine. Leave them for about one hour. After an hour, use a thermometer to check the temperature of the cup of water and the cup of sand. Is the sand hotter? How much hotter is it?

Watch the smoke rise in a chimney. Can you explain why the smoke moves up the chimney and why fresh air keeps moving into the chimney?

III. The Greenhouse Effect

An increase in the concentration or amount of carbon dioxide in the air may cause the surface temperature of the earth to rise. This effect of increasing surface temperature due to gases in the atmosphere is called the greenhouse effect.

Modern industry and technology have improved our lives, but they also have caused the amount of carbon dioxide in the atmosphere to increase dramatically. Coal, oil, and natural gas are types of fossil fuels that are used to heat buildings, power factories, and run cars and trucks. Burning fossil fuels causes carbon from the coal, oil, or natural gas to combine with oxygen in the air to produce carbon dioxide. More carbon dioxide in the air may lead to the greenhouse effect.

Other greenhouse gases include chlorofluorocarbons used in refrigeration and air conditioning, nitrogen oxide caused by pollution, and methane produced in the guts of cows and termites. Greenhouse gases can prevent heat from being radiated or going back into space from the earth. If this excess heat from the sun does not go back into space, it can cause warmer temperatures on the earth's surface.

An increase in global temperature due to the greenhouse effect could have major environmental effects on the earth. Sea level could rise due to the melting of polar ice. A rising sea level would cause flooding of coastal areas where many people live. In addition, the warming of the earth surface could cause changes in weather patterns, leading to more violent storms such as tornadoes and hurricanes. Also, some areas of the earth would become hotter and drier and crops would not grow as well, which could result in shortages of food.

In the following experiments, you will learn more about the causes and possible effects of greenhouse warming.

Experiment #5

Can Glass Jars Be Used to Show the Greenhouse Effect?

Materials

Two large, clear glass jars
Outdoor thermometer

Procedure

On a sunny day, set one glass jar on the ground so that the sun is shining on it. Put a thermometer inside the glass jar so that the thermometer scale is facing the sun and you can easily read it. Now turn the second glass jar upside down and put it on top of the first jar. The thermometer should now be inside the two glass jars.

Leave the glass jars and thermometer in the sun for about one hour. After an hour, look at the thermometer. Now remove the top jar. Wait a few minutes, and check the temperature on the thermometer again. Now remove the thermometer from the jar. Set the thermometer outside the jar with the sun still shining on it. Wait several minutes, and check the temperature again.

Observations

What is the temperature on the thermometer inside the

glass jars? What is the temperature after the top jar is removed? What is the temperature after the thermometer is placed outside the bottom jar?

Discussion

When sunlight passes through the atmosphere to reach the surface of the earth, solar energy is absorbed by water and land. A thermometer in the sun will be hotter than the air temperature because of the solar energy striking the thermometer.

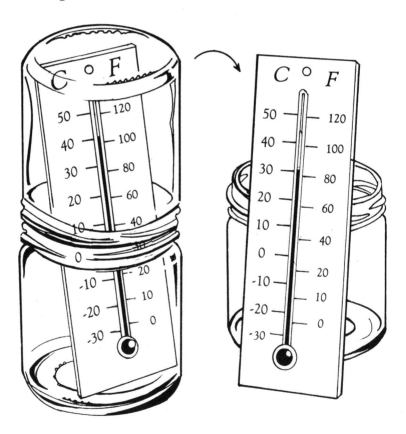

Solar energy reaching the earth causes the surface of the earth to become warmer. However, the water and land and everything on the earth give off or radiate some heat back to the atmosphere. Some of this extra heat energy goes out into space. Some of the heat energy is trapped by the earth's atmosphere. The trapping of this extra heat is called the greenhouse effect.

The temperature inside the two glass jars should become higher than the outside air temperature. Heat energy is trapped inside the glass jars. These two jars are like a miniature greenhouse. The infrared radiation that we feel as heat on our skin on a warm sunny day passes through the glass jars. Also, solar energy from visible light passes through the jars. However, the radiated heat from objects inside the glass jars does not have as much energy, and this heat is trapped by the glass. This trapped heat causes an increase in the temperature inside the two jars.

When the top jar is removed, the temperature should drop because there is less trapped heat. Heat escapes from the open jar. When the thermometer is removed from the jar, the temperature should drop more. With the thermometer outside the jars, there is nothing to trap the heat.

The greenhouse effect is important to maintain the temperature of the surface of the earth. Without the natural greenhouse effect caused by water vapor and carbon dioxide gas in the air, the earth would be too cold for life. However, too much carbon dioxide can trap too much heat and cause the earth to be too warm.

From studies of gases trapped in ice in ancient glaciers, scientists have determined the amount of carbon dioxide present in the air during earlier times in the earth's history. During the ice ages when the earth's surface was cold, the amount of carbon dioxide was about 200 parts per million (2 parts per 10,000). This means that out of every one million gas molecules in the air approximately 200 were carbon dioxide molecules. Between the ice ages when the earth's climate was warmer, the amount of carbon dioxide was about 280 parts per million. In other words, more carbon dioxide in the air is associated with higher temperatures on the surface of the earth.

Since 1958 scientists have measured the amount of carbon dioxide in the air on a mountain top in Hawaii. From 1958 to 1990, the amount of carbon dioxide in the air has increased from 315 to more than 350 parts per million.

Carbon dioxide has increased to more than 350 parts per million because of modern industrialization. The burning of fossil fuels such as coal, oil, and natural gas, as well as the clearing and burning of trees, has caused an increase in the carbon dioxide in the air.

Other Things to Try

Fill two identical jars each half full with water. Screw the top tightly on one jar. Leave the second jar open with no top. Take both jars outside on a warm sunny day. Turn the jar with the top upside down. Set this jar upside down on the ground so more sun can shine through the glass. Set the second, open jar down beside the first jar. Leave both jars in the sun for about one hour. After an hour, use a thermometer to compare the temperature of the water in the two jars. Can you explain any differences in the water temperature?

Use a thermometer to check the temperature of a closed car that has been parked with the sun shining on it for several hours. Roll down the windows. Wait about thirty minutes, and then check the temperature again. Has the car gotten cooler? Can you explain why?

If you are ever inside a greenhouse at a garden store or florist's shop, try to feel if it is warmer inside the greenhouse or outside? Are the roof and walls made of glass or plastic that you can see through? Can the sunlight pass through the walls or roof to warm the plants and pots and soil inside? What happens to the heat given off by the things inside the greenhouse?

Experiment #6

Can Absorbing Sunlight Trap Heat Energy?

Materials

Six ice cubes
Dark dirt
White sand
Two paper plates

Procedure

Go outside on a warm day and put the two paper plates in a sunny spot. Spread a layer of dark dirt on the center of one plate. Spread a layer of white sand on the center of the other plate. Put three ice cubes on the dirt and three ice cubes on the white sand. Use ice cubes that are nearly identical in size.

Look at the ice cubes every few minutes until they all melt. Compare the size of the ice cubes as they are melting.

Observations

Do some of the ice cubes melt faster than others? Does the ice on the dirt melt faster? Does the ice on the sand melt faster?

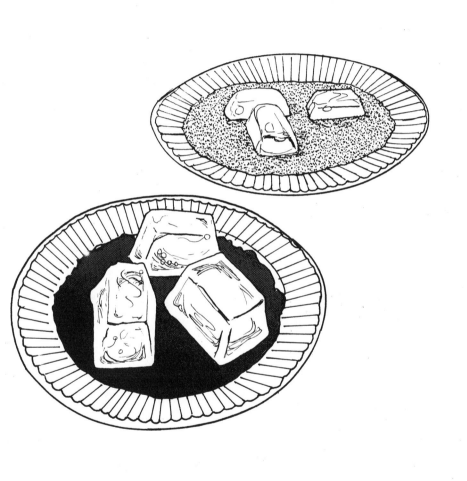

Discussion

The ability of a surface to reflect light is called its albedo. Snow and ice have a high albedo. Snow and ice reflect sunlight. Dirt and dark ground do not reflect light but absorb sunlight. Dirt and dark ground have a low albedo.

You probably saw that the ice cubes placed on the black dirt disappeared slower than the ice cubes placed on the white sand. The ice cubes on top of the sand melted faster because the sand has a higher albedo. The white sand reflected heat energy back to the ice cubes and caused them to melt faster.

The albedo has an important part in the greenhouse effect that controls the earth's temperature. Light from the sun warms the surface of the earth. Land and water radiate or give up a certain amount of heat energy back to the air. Some of this heat energy goes back into outer space, but some is trapped by greenhouse gases like carbon dioxide.

If too much heat is trapped, the earth's surface will get warmer. If an increase in carbon dioxide and other greenhouse gases in the atmosphere cause the earth's temperature to warm, then snow and ice on the ground will melt. If more snow and ice melt, the earth's albedo will decrease because the reflective snow and ice will be gone. The dark ground underneath has a lower albedo and will absorb more sunlight heat energy. If more heat is absorbed, then the earth's temperature could increase more, and this will cause even more snow and ice to melt. Decreasing the albedo or light reflectiveness of the earth could cause greenhouse warming to be worse.

Other Things to Try

Try this experiment with pieces of ice placed on aluminum foil and ice placed on the ground. Does the ice on the aluminum foil melt faster because the foil reflects the light?

Compare how long it takes for ice to melt that has been put on a dark plastic plate and a white plastic plate.

Try sprinkling pepper on top of a piece of ice and see if it melts faster. Dark pepper on top of the ice may absorb heat energy from the sunlight and cause the ice to melt faster than uncovered ice. Would you expect dirty snow or clean white snow to melt faster?

Experiment #7

Could Greenhouse Warming Affect the Level of the Ocean?

Materials

A large apple	Water
A knife	A measuring cup
Ice cubes	

A two-cup glass measuring cup

Procedure

Have an adult cut an apple in half. Push the apple, flat side down, into the bottom of the large glass measuring cup. The apple should be pushed down hard enough so that it is stuck firmly in the bottom of the measuring cup. Add one cup of ice cubes to the top of the apple. Add enough water so that only the top third of the apple is above the water. This will represent land. The ice cubes will be piled on top of the apple. Wait for all the ice to melt and then check the level of the water.

Pour the water out of the large measuring cup and remove the apple. Now add one cup of ice cubes to the large glass measuring cup. Fill with water to bring the water level up to exactly the one cup mark. Wait for all the ice to melt and then check the level of the water.

Observations

Did the level of the water rise when the ice melted in the first experiment? Did the level of the water rise when the ice melted in the second experiment?

Discussion

The trapping of heat near the earth is called the greenhouse effect. The greenhouse effect helps control the temperature of the earth so it does not become too cold. However, the amount of carbon dioxide is increasing in our atmosphere due to the burning of coal, oil, natural gas, and gasoline. This increase in carbon dioxide as well as other greenhouse gases, such as chlorofluorocarbons (used in air conditioners), could trap too much heat and cause the earth to become warmer.

In your first experiment, you should have seen a rise in the water level when the ice that was on top of the apple melted. The apple may have become covered with water just as land near the sea may become covered with water if the earth's temperature rises too much.

In your second experiment, you should not see any rise in the water level from the floating ice. When floating ice melts, the liquid water formed takes the place of the ice that was under water and so there is no increase in the water level.

A warmer earth could cause ice to melt in the earth's polar regions. You have shown in your experiment that floating ice such as icebergs will not cause the sea level to rise even if they melt. However, there are other sources of ice, such as glaciers, that are on land and not floating. If this ice melts, low land along the coast could be covered with water all around the world. This process might be slow; but if the ocean level rises, a large number of people could lose their homes, and land used to grow crops would be destroyed.

Other Things to Try

Repeat this experiment with different amounts of ice and water. Compare your results.

Add one cup of ice cubes to the large measuring cup. Fill with water until all the ice cubes are floating. How much of the ice is out of the water and how much of the ice is under the water? Can you see why floating ice does not change the water level when it melts?

Look at a map of the world and see how many large cities you can find that are close to the coast. How would these cities be affected by rising sea levels?

Experiment #8

Is Carbon Dioxide Held in Water?

Materials

A clear, carbonated drink in a plastic bottle

Procedure

Remove the label from the bottle so you can more easily see inside the bottle. The bottle should not be cold but should be the same temperature as the room.

Look at the liquid in the unopened bottle. Try squeezing the bottle. Unscrew the bottle cap and watch the liquid for about twenty seconds. Squeeze the bottle again. Screw the cap back on the bottle and observe the liquid once again.

Observations

Do you see bubbles in the liquid before the bottle is opened? Do you see bubbles in the liquid after the bottle is opened? What happens to the bubbles when the bottle is closed? Does the bottle feel firmer when it is opened or unopened?

Discussion

In a carbonated drink, carbon dioxide is dissolved in water. The pressure of carbon dioxide above the liquid causes extra carbon dioxide molecules to go into the water. When the bottle is capped, some carbon dioxide and some water molecules are trapped above the liquid. The pressure of these gases inside the bottle is about two or three times greater than the pressure of air in the room. The greater pressure when the bottle is capped causes a closed bottle to feel much firmer than an opened bottle.

When the bottle is opened, you may be able to hear the gas as it rushes from the top of the bottle to mix with the air in the room. You should see bubbles of gas

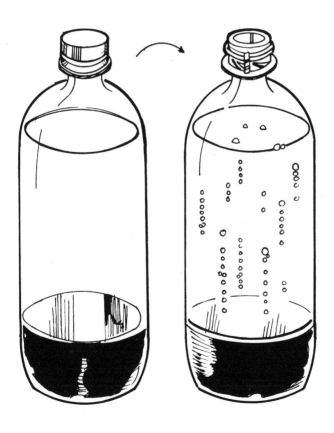

forming in the liquid and rising to the top of the bottle. This is the extra carbon dioxide leaving the liquid.

When you cap the bottle, the pressure of gas increases above the liquid until bubbles stop forming. When the bubbles stop forming, a new equilibrium or balance is reached between the carbon dioxide in the water and the carbon dioxide in the space above the water. In an equilibrium, there are some carbon dioxide molecules leaving the liquid but just as many other carbon dioxide molecules going back into the liquid.

You may be able to repeat this process several times allowing some carbon dioxide to escape and a new equilibrium to form.

Extra carbon dioxide is going into our atmosphere because of burning fossil fuels such as coal, oil, and gasoline. However, some of this extra carbon dioxide dissolves in the oceans. There is an equilibrium between the carbon dioxide in the air and the carbon dioxide dissolved in the oceans and other bodies of water. As more carbon dioxide is put into the air, this equilibrium is changed.

Some carbon dioxide is removed from the atmosphere because carbon dioxide dissolves in water. In fact, the ocean may store about sixty times more carbon than the atmosphere.

Calcium carbonate is used to make shells and skeletons. Some of these shells and skeletons settle to the bottom of the ocean and are stored in the sand and sediment at the bottom of the ocean.

As carbon dioxide is used in calcium carbonate in marine animal shells and skeletons, the equilibrium is shifted, and more carbon dioxide is removed from the air. The equilibrium between carbon dioxide in the air and in the oceans is one that helps keep our environment from changing too rapidly and helps maintain a balance in nature.

Tiny microscopic plants called photosynthetic plankton live in the ocean. These plants use sunlight and carbon dioxide dissolved in ocean water to make larger carbon-containing molecules. As these plankton are eaten by other animals, the large carbon-containing molecules are used for food by other animals.

Other Things to Try

Repeat this experiment with a bottle taken from the refrigerator and see if more or less carbon dioxide comes out of a cold carbonated beverage. Temperature changes can change the equilibrium. More carbon dioxide should dissolve in cold water than in warm water.

An increase in carbon dioxide in the atmosphere could contribute to the warming of the earth due to the greenhouse effect. This warming could cause less carbon dioxide to dissolve in the ocean, and this could make the greenhouse effect even worse. See if you can demonstrate this effect by observing whether less carbon dioxide bubbles out of a warm or cold soft drink bottle.

About half the carbon dioxide added to the atmosphere from burning fossil fuels and destroying the forests has been taken up by the ocean rather than staying in the air. If the ocean and marine animals did not help remove carbon dioxide from the air, the warming due to the greenhouse effect would be much worse.

Repeat this experiment allowing some carbon dioxide to escape and a new equilibrium to form. Now, screw the cap back on the bottle. Do you still see bubbles of carbon dioxide? Look at the liquid in the closed bottle. Unscrew the bottle cap and watch the liquid for about twenty seconds. Screw the cap back on the bottle and observe the liquid once again.

Try this experiment with a bottle that has been opened many times. Do bubbles form when the bottle is opened? Do you see bubbles in the liquid after the bottle is opened?

IV. Air Pollution and Ozone

Air pollution is caused by the release of chemical substances into the atmosphere that are not normally found in the atmosphere. There are many sources of air pollution, both human and natural. One way people cause air pollution is by burning fossil fuels (such as heating oil, gasoline, natural gas, and coal).

Forest fires, volcanic eruptions, and soil erosion are examples of natural sources of air pollution. Rain, wind, and gravity naturally clean the air of pollutants, but with the increased use of fossil fuels, pollutants have been added into the air faster than natural forces can remove them.

Air pollution can be harmful in many ways. It can cause health problems for people and animals. It can damage plants and reduce crop harvests. It can cause damage to buildings, clothing, and other objects. Air pollution can make the air smell bad and can make things dirty.

Ozone, a form of oxygen, can be an air pollutant. When it is found in the upper atmosphere, it acts as a protector of the earth by absorbing harmful ultraviolet radiation from the sun. However, when ozone is found in the lower atmosphere, it acts as a harmful pollutant. Ozone can aggravate heart and lung diseases in people and animals and can kill many types of plants.

The ozone layer in the upper atmosphere is currently in danger. Since the late 1970s, scientists have observed the yearly disappearance of ozone in the upper atmosphere over the Antarctic. This annual loss of ozone over Antarctica creates what is called the ozone hole. One cause of this loss is thought to be chlorofluorocarbons (CFC's). CFC's are used in refrigerators and air conditioners. Even when the use of CFC's is banned, the loss of ozone in the upper atmosphere may continue to be a problem for years to come.

Today, efforts are being made by governments, companies, and individuals to reduce the amount of air pollution. This is being accomplished by finding ways to burn fossil fuels more cleanly, by removing pollutants from burning fossil fuels before they reach the atmosphere, and by developing alternative energy sources such as solar, wind, water, geothermal, and nuclear energy. Another way is simply energy conservation. In the following experiments, you will learn more about air pollution and ozone.

Experiment #9

What Is the Effect of a Thermal Inversion on Air Pollution?

Materials

Two small glass bottles   Ice

A metal saucepan   Plastic bowl

Water   Matches

Stove

Procedure

ASK AN ADULT TO HELP YOU WITH THIS EXPERI-
MENT. DO NOT USE THE STOVE BY YOURSELF. DO
NOT USE THE MATCHES BY YOURSELF.

Fill a metal saucepan about half full with water. Heat
the pan of water on a stove until the water just begins
to boil. Turn off the stove.

Fill a plastic bowl full of ice. Now stand a small glass
bottle in the bowl of ice. Set the second glass bottle so
that it is standing in the pan of hot water. Wait about ten
minutes to give the air in the bottles time to cool or
warm.

Light a match and drop it in the cold bottle. Light a
second match and drop it in the hot bottle. Watch the
smoke that forms in each bottle.

Observations

Does the smoke rise out of the hot bottle? Does the smoke rise out of the cold bottle? Which bottle keeps its smoke the longest?

Discussion

Normally the air near the ground is warmer than the air higher in the atmosphere. The warm air near the ground rises because warm air is less dense or lighter than cold air. The warm air rises, and the heavier cold air falls toward the ground.

The air in the hot bottle is warmer than the air in the room. You should see the smoke in the warm bottle rise with its hot air into the room.

The air in the cold bottle is cooler than the air in the room. The smoke in the cold air tends to stay in the bottle rather than rise into the air. The smoke should clear from the bottle with warm air much faster than the bottle with cold air.

This process of warm air rising and cold air falling keeps the air moving and helps carry pollution away from its source. Cars and factories in cities produce certain pollution molecules such as ozone, hydrocarbons, carbon monoxide, and nitrogen oxide. Rising air helps carry these molecules away from the cities.

Some cities such as Los Angeles frequently have thermal inversions form. A thermal inversion occurs when hot air is above colder air. Hot air rises, and cold air falls. However, if the cold air is nearer the ground, there will be no mixing of air. This still air has no wind to carry away pollution particles. A thermal inversion traps air near the ground.

Pollution molecules build up in the air if there is no wind to carry them away from the city or rain to wash them out of air. This can sometimes lead to deadly results. In Donora, a small town in Pennsylvania, in October 1948, 6,000 people in a town of 14,000 got sick, and 20 died from pollution and a smog that was so thick people couldn't see across the street. Smog is a combination of smoke and fog.

Many pollution molecules you cannot see. However, sometimes you may see smoke combine with fog to produce smog.

Estimates of deaths from pollution caused by still air and a build-up of smog and pollution include 650 people in London in 1873, 400 people in New York City in 1963, and 4,000 people in London in 1952 during five days of smog!

We cannot control the weather or prevent thermal inversions from occurring, but we can reduce the pollution that causes smog. We can drive more fuel-efficient cars (cars that get more miles per gallon of gasoline). We can use devices to help stop pollution molecules from being released from cars, factories, and power plants.

Other Things to Try

Repeat this experiment using a bottle that is the temperature of the room air. Does this smoke clear faster or slower than the smoke in the hot bottle? Does this smoke clear faster or slower than the smoke in the cold bottle?

Use a watch or clock, and check the amount of smoke in each bottle every minute. How long does it take for the smoke to clear from the bottle with the warm air? How long does it take for all the smoke to clear from the bottle with the cold air?

Try to observe factories, plants, or trucks near where you live. Can you see smoke being given off from any of these. White clouds may just be harmless water vapor, but darker black smoke contains dust and pollution. Darkness of smoke is sometimes used as a measure of air pollution. The area where you live may have a group of people called an air pollution control board or air pollution agency who help to monitor pollution. If you observe continuous dark smoke from a chimney or smokestack, you may wish to report it to your local air pollution agency.

Depending on where you live, you may actually be able to see smog hanging in the air over a city near you.

Experiment #10

Can Pollution Harm Clothing?

Materials

Two small pieces of rayon cloth (if you cannot find
a scrap piece of clothing made of rayon, you can
purchase small pieces of rayon at a fabric store)
Fingernail polish remover
A cotton ball
A clear glass jar with a tight fitting lid
Tape
Scissors

Procedure

ASK AN ADULT TO HELP YOU WITH THIS EXPERI-
MENT. YOU SHOULD NOT USE FINGERNAIL POLISH
BY YOURSELF. FINGERNAIL POLISH IS FLAMMABLE.
DO NOT USE IT NEAR A FLAME OR HEAT SOURCE.

Ask an adult to soak a cotton ball with fingernail
polish remover. Ask the adult to place the cotton ball in
the glass jar. Tighten the lid.

Use the scissors to cut two pieces of rayon fabric
about 2.5 cm (1 inch) by 5 cm (2 inches). Remove the lid
from the glass jar. Tape one end of a piece of the rayon
fabric to the inside of the lid. Retighten the lid on the jar
making sure all of the rayon fabric goes into the jar. Do

not let the rayon fabric touch the cotton ball or the bottom of the jar. Set the jar in a place where it will not be disturbed. Set the second piece of rayon fabric beside the jar.

Remove the piece of rayon fabric from the jar after three hours. Pull on the rayon fabric with your hands. Pull on the piece of rayon fabric that was not placed in the jar. If the piece of rayon fabric that was in the jar does not tear easily, put it back in the jar and leave it there overnight. The next day remove it from the jar and pull on it.

To clean up, rinse the cotton ball and the jar with water from a sink faucet for thirty seconds. Throw the cotton ball in the trash.

Observations

Does the piece of rayon fabric in the jar look different after it is removed from the jar? Does this piece of rayon fabric tear more easily than the piece left beside the jar? When you pull on the piece of rayon fabric that was in the jar, does it feel sticky?

Discussion

In this experiment, you are using fingernail polish remover to study how air pollution from hydrocarbons (one of the components of smog) can damage clothing. Most fingernail polish removers contain the chemical substance acetone mixed with water. Acetone is a hydrocarbon that also contains oxygen. Acetone is a liquid and is used as a solvent for cleaning. A solvent is a material that dissolves other materials.

In the experiment, the acetone on the cotton ball evaporates and the jar fills with acetone vapors. The acetone vapors attack the rayon fibers in the cloth by dissolving the chemical substances that make the rayon fibers. When you pull on this piece of rayon fiber, you should see that it tears easily. The piece of rayon fiber that was not attacked by the acetone vapors should not tear as easily.

Smog, which means smoke and fog, is a major air pollution problem for many cities of the world. Smog can be harmful to animals and plants, and it can damage material objects. It can also make it more difficult for airplane pilots and automobile and truck drivers to see.

There are two basic types of smog. Both are a mixture of air pollutants and water vapor.

The first type is called acid smog. Acid smog contains sulfur dioxide, sulfuric acid, and soot particles. Acid smog can be found around areas where coal is burned.

The second type of smog is called photochemical smog and is caused mainly by automobile exhaust. This type of smog is called photochemical smog because light from the sun is needed to make some of the pollutants. Photochemical smog contains mostly nitrogen oxides, carbon monoxide, ozone, and unburned hydrocarbons. (Hydrocarbons are compounds containing carbon and hydrogen atoms.)

The ozone in photochemical smog is formed by sunlight shining on nitrogen oxides and oxygen in the air. Sunlight and oxygen can also change the unburned hydrocarbons into chemical substances that are irritating to the lungs and eyes.

Hydrocarbons are released into the air in urban areas

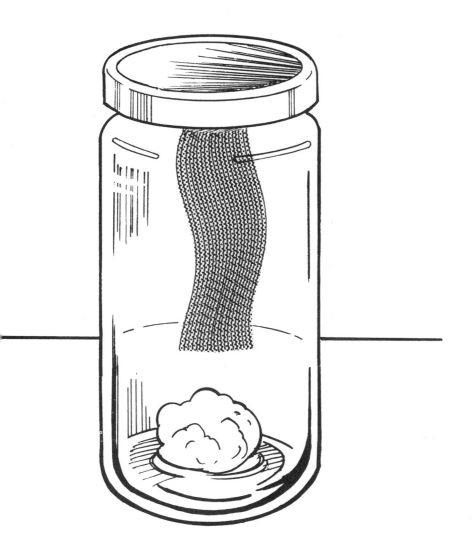

by ways other than automobile exhaust. Some common examples of hydrocarbons used in urban areas are gasoline, paint thinner, and industrial solvents like acetone. These hydrocarbon materials can get in the air because they evaporate easily. When a substance evaporates, it changes from liquid to a gas or vapor.

Hydrocarbons also get into the air from natural sources. Some natural sources of hydrocarbons are trees, swamps, and ruminant animals like cows.

Other Things to Try

Carefully remove the bottom of a clean, empty food can with a can opener. Tightly stretch a piece of nylon hose around one end of the can. Use a piece of string or tape to hold the nylon hose to the can. Place the can with the nylon hose facing up in a location outside where it will not be disturbed for a month. Each week for a month, look at the hose for tiny particles and broken threads.

Nylon is a synthetic fabric that is sensitive to acid pollutants. Acid pollutants can cause the tiny fibers in nylon to break apart.

Experiment #11

Can Weather
Affect Air Pollution?

Materials

A piece of notebook paper

Fourteen small pieces of paper (about
two inches square)

A pan

The Air Quality Index for each day for two weeks

Procedure

Try to do this experiment in the summer when there will
be some hot, hazy, sunny days.

You will need the Air Quality Index or AQI for each
day for two weeks. The AQI can be found in the weather
section of most large newspapers. Also, some television
and radio stations give the day's AQI during the
weather segment of their broadcasts. You may also try
contacting a weatherperson or your local pollution
board directly for help in finding the AQI for your area.

The AQI may be reported as either a number from
zero to five hundred or as one of five categories. The five
possible categories are good, moderate, unhealthful,
very unhealthful, and hazardous. The relationship

between the five categories and the number values of AQI is shown in the figure below.

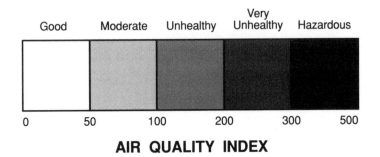

AIR QUALITY INDEX

Use the pen to draw two crossing lines that divide the piece of notebook paper into four equal blocks. Label one block "good," a second block "moderate," a third block "unhealthful," and the fourth block "very unhealthful and hazardous."

On the first day of the experiment, write on a small piece of paper the day's date, the AQI for that day, and the general weather conditions for the day (Was the day sunny and hot or cool? Was there much wind that day? Was there any rain that day?). Place this piece of paper in the appropriate block on the piece of notebook paper. Repeat this process for thirteen more days.

Observations

Does the AQI in your area change from day to day? Does a change in the weather change your AQI? Is your AQI on a windless, hot, sunny day different than on a rainy or windy day?

Discussion

The Air Quality Index or AQI is a measure of the amount of air pollution. Seven major air pollutants are used to determine the AQI. These pollutants are carbon monoxide, sulfur oxides, nitrogen oxides, particulate matter, ozone, hydrocarbons, and lead.

The AQI ranges in value from 0 to 500 in five categories as shown in the figure below. The United States Environmental Protection Agency has set an AQI of 100 as the standard for judging air quality. The official name of this standard is the National Ambient Air Quality

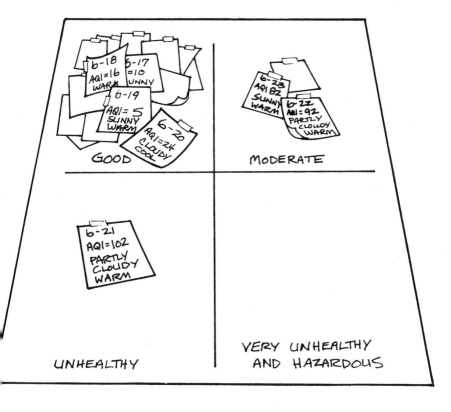

Standard. According to this standard, with an AQI value below 100, no adverse health effects should be observed. Caution should be used when the AQI is between 101 and 199. An AQI between 200 and 299 is considered very unhealthful, and people are advised to stay indoors. An AQI between 300 and 500 is hazardous, and all people are to stay inside their homes or other buildings.

In the summer, the pollutant ozone is the major contributor to the AQI for most cities. Ozone is a form of oxygen. Ozone is formed by the action of sunlight on pollutants from the exhaust of motor vehicles and oxygen in the air. Ozone can cause health problems for humans and animals, and it can damage plants.

On a sunny, windless day, the amount of ozone in the air usually increases. Rain helps wash ozone and other pollutants out of the air. Wind helps scatter ozone and other pollutants. You should observe in your chart that on a hot, calm summer day, the AQI is higher than on a rainy day.

Other Things to Try

Repeat this experiment during other times of the year. Do you get similar results?

Experiment #12

Can You Make and Smell Ozone?

Materials

A battery-powered small toy car (available at most toy shops or discount stores)

Procedure

Remove the cover so that you can see the car's motor. Smell around the area of the motor. Try to remember this smell.

Turn on the car while you hold it. The motor should now be running. Smell around the area of the motor after the motor has been running for fifteen seconds.

Observations

Does the area around the motor of the car smell different after the motor has run for fifteen seconds? How would you describe this smell? Is the smell earthy or fresh-smelling?

Discussion

Ozone is a form of oxygen that contains three oxygen atoms bound together in a single molecule. The major form of oxygen consists of two oxygen atoms combined together as a molecule. This form of oxygen is called diatomic oxygen or simply oxygen.

Ozone is a pollutant in the lower atmosphere because it is a chemical substance out of place in the environment. Ozone is made in the lower atmosphere from other air pollutants known as nitrogen oxides. Nitrogen oxides are molecules made of nitrogen and oxygen atoms. Nitrogen oxides can be produced during the combustion of fuels such as gasoline and diesel fuel

in automobiles, trucks, and airplanes. It can also be made during the burning of coal. The nitrogen oxide known as nitrogen dioxide can undergo a chemical reaction with oxygen molecules in the presence of sunlight to produce ozone.

Since more cars are driven during daylight, the amount of nitrogen oxides, and thus the amount of ozone in the lower atmosphere, is greater during the day than at night. Ozone can be particularly bad on sunny, windless days because it stays close to the ground. Wind and rain help remove ozone from the air.

Ozone is also made in the lower atmosphere by lightning during thunderstorms. The electricity of a lightning bolt causes molecules of diatomic oxygen to rearrange into molecules of ozone. Have you ever noticed that the air smells particularly fresh after a thunderstorm? The fresh smell is due in part to the presence of ozone. Ozone in small amounts has a fresh or earthy smell. In large amounts, ozone has a sharp, pungent smell.

In this experiment you are using electricity to make ozone. When a battery powered car is run at high speed, electricity can arc in the electric motor. This arcing or discharge of electricity can cause diatomic oxygen around the motor to rearrange into ozone. The motor should have a fresh or earthy smell if ozone is present.

Other Things to Try

Another way to do this experiment is with an electric car or train set. You may find the odor of ozone stronger with an electric car or train set.

The procedure is written for an electric car. You will do the same thing if you have an electric train.

Before you turn on the power to the car's track, smell around the area of the motor of the electric car. Try to remember this smell.

Place the electric car on its track. Hold the car so it does not move. You do not want to race the car around the track in this experiment. Turn on the electric power to the car track and run the electric motor in the car on high for ten seconds. Turn off the power to the track and immediately smell around the area of the motor of the electric car.

Sometimes it is possible to smell the ozone that can be a major part of your air pollution in the summertime. To try this, go out into a field or on top of a mountain on a hot, hazy, windless summer day. If the air is earthy- or fresh-smelling, you may be smelling ozone.

V. Dust

Dust is made of tiny solid particles that are held or suspended in air. Dust has many natural and human sources. Some natural sources include volcanic eruptions, erosion of soil, salt spray from oceans, forest fires, and even particles from outer space that penetrate the earth's atmosphere. Some examples of human sources of dust include the burning of fossil fuels, plowing fields, making cloth, erasing pencil marks, and even walking on the sidewalk. In fact, everyday wear and tear on materials we use makes dust.

Dust is both helpful and harmful to the environment. Dust allows drops of water and ice crystals to form in the atmosphere, causing rain or snow, and dust can also cause beautiful sunsets, such as those caused by a belt of dust encircling the earth from the volcanic eruptions of Mount Pinatubo in the Philippines in June 1991.

Dust can also be a harmful type of pollution, containing particles that are unhealthy to breathe. It has been shown that industrial areas can be three to four times more dusty than rural areas. An industrial area may contain over fifty million dust particles in a space about the size of your fist.

Also, too much dust can block the sun's light from reaching earth and settle on plant leaves, depriving plants of the energy they need to live. It is important for us to understand the many effects dust has on the environment. In the following experiments, you will learn more about dust and how it affects the environment.

Experiment #13

Are More Dust Particles in the Air Outside or Inside?

Materials

Three pieces of paper
Clear tape
A magnifying glass
A pen

Procedure

Write "outside" on one piece of paper, "inside" on a second piece of paper, and "inside drawer" on the third piece of paper. Tear a piece of clear tape about four inches long. Overlap one end with the other by about one half of an inch and press the ends together to seal. You should now have a circle of tape with the sticky side facing out. Attach and flatten this piece of tape to the first piece of paper. Do the same thing to the second and third pieces of paper. Now each piece of paper has tape attached to it.

Place the piece of paper labeled "outside" outdoors in a place where it will not be disturbed. Place a heavy object on the paper to keep wind from possibly blowing the paper away. Move the piece of paper labeled "outside" inside if you think it is going to rain. Return the paper outside when the chance of rain disappears.

Place the piece of paper labeled "inside" in a spot in your room where it will not be disturbed. Finally, place the piece of paper labeled "inside drawer" in a drawer that will not be disturbed. Close the drawer.

Observe the pieces of tape on each piece of paper each day for a week. You may want to use a magnifying glass to get a closer look at each piece of tape.

Observations

Which piece of tape contains the most dust particles after one day? Which piece of tape contains the most dust particles after one week? What colors are the dust particles? What kind of sizes and shapes do the dust particles have? Do the dust particles trapped outdoors look like the dust particles trapped inside the house?

Discussion

Natural sources of dust in the atmosphere include volcanic eruptions, erosion of soil, salt spray from oceans, forest fires, plant spores, bacteria, and dust particles from outer space that penetrate the earth's atmosphere.

Humans also create dust that goes into the air. The burning of fossil fuels produces soot and fly ash. Burning wood produces ash. Plowing fields puts soil in the air. Rubber particles are added to the air from automobile and truck tires rubbing against roads. Tiny fibers are added to the air from clothes rubbing together. Even walking on a concrete sidewalk puts dust in the air. Whenever two solid substances rub or grind together, dust can be made.

Dust particles come in many shapes and sizes. Dust fibers are rodlike. Plant spores are usually spherical. Soot particles can be spherical or rodlike. Mineral, soil, and metal dust is granular. Dust from salt spray looks

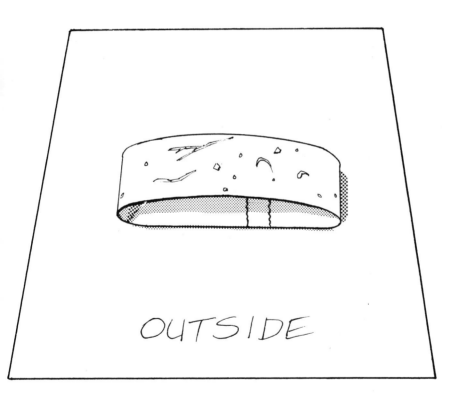

OUTSIDE

like a cube. Do you see any of these shapes on your pieces of tape?

Dust particles range in size from particles large enough to see with your eye to particles that can only be seen with the most powerful of microscopes. To be classified as dust, a particle cannot be larger than 1/16 of a millimeter (a dime is about 1 mm thick). It would take 16,000 dust particles, each 1/16 of a millimeter in size, placed side by side to have a line of dust particles one meter long. However, most dust particles are smaller than this.

In this experiment, you will probably see more dust particles trapped on the piece of tape on the paper labeled "outside." Normally, there are more dust particles in the air outside than inside. The piece of tape that was placed in a drawer should contain the fewest number of dust particles.

Other Things to Try

Prepare four pieces of paper with tape as described in the procedure above. Write "kitchen" on one piece, "bedroom" on another piece, "living room" on a third piece, and "bathroom" on the fourth piece. Place these pieces of paper in the rooms labeled on the paper. Observe the pieces of tape each day for a week. Do some rooms in your house contain more dust than others? Do dust particles from different rooms look the same or different?

Find a dusty surface around your room. A good place to look is the top of a bookcase or the top of a picture frame. Wipe the dusty surface with a white facial tissue. Look at the dust particles with the magnifying glass. Describe what you see.

Use a magnifying glass to look at the dust on a window ledge or window seal that is outside. Most of the dust found on the outside surface of buildings is soot.

Experiment #14

Why Is the Sky Blue and a Sunset Red?

Materials

A bright flashlight	A measuring cup
Nonfat dry milk	A tall clear glass
A measuring spoon	Water

Procedure

Add one cup of water to the tall clear glass. Add one-quarter teaspoon of instant nonfat dry milk to the water. Stir the milk and water with the measuring spoon. Observe the color of the milky solution.

Take the flashlight and the glass of milky water into a dark room. Turn on the flashlight and shine the light through the bottom of the glass. You may need to put the flashlight against the glass. Look through the side of the glass. Observe the color of the light. Look through the top of the glass down at the flashlight. Observe the color of the light.

Observations

Is the milk and water solution clear or cloudy? Does the milk and water solution have a slight bluish color? Is the light beam slightly bluish in color when you observe the light beam from the side of the glass?

Is the flashlight bulb red-orange in color when you look at it through the top of the glass of milky water?

Discussion

In this experiment you are using a glass of milky water to simulate the atmosphere and to study how light is affected by particles. You will show why the sky is blue and a sunset is red and orange.

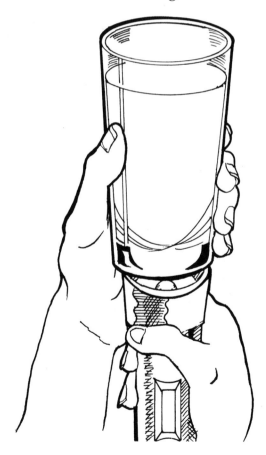

Light from the sun and light from a light bulb contain all the colors of the rainbow. These colors are violet, indigo, blue, green, yellow, orange and red. White light is the name given to light that contains all these colors.

The earth's atmosphere is a complex mixture of gases. The atmosphere also contains dust particles that are light enough to be suspended or held in the air. Dust is also called "suspended particulate matter." The gases in air are mostly molecules of nitrogen and oxygen. Air also contains some water molecules and carbon dioxide molecules.

Light from the sun is changed when it passes through the earth's atmosphere. The sun's light is scattered by the air molecules and dust particles in the atmosphere. When light is scattered, it goes in many different directions.

Some colors of white light can be scattered more than others. Blue light is scattered more than other colors in white light by air molecules and tiny dust particles. The blue light moves in all directions when it is scattered. This is why a clear sky appears bright and blue during the day. If none of the sun's light was scattered, the sky would appear black. This is why objects in photos made in outer space appear to be on a black background.

If air is particularly dusty or if air contains large dust particles or crystals of ice, then the sky appears more bluish white. Large particles can scatter other colors in white light. When several different colors of light are scattered, the light appears more white.

Red light is scattered the least of all the colors in white light. Most of the red light from the sun passes through the atmosphere directly. At sunset the sun and the surrounding sky appears red or orange because we are viewing the sun more directly. This means we are viewing a more direct beam of light from the sun. Since the blue light of the sun is scattered by the atmosphere and little reaches our eyes, the sun's light appears reddish.

In this experiment, when white light from the flashlight passes through the milky water, the light is scattered by groups of large molecules in the milk. These protein molecules scatter the light from the flashlight like air molecules and dust particles scatter the sun's light. The blue light is scattered more than the other colors. This is why milky water looks slightly bluish. Red light is scattered the least of all the colors. This is why the flashlight light bulb should appear reddish when you look at it directly through the milky water.

Other Things to Try

Repeat this experiment by adding less or more instant nonfat dry milk. What do you observe?

Experiment #15

Are There Solid Particles in Smoke?

Materials

A match
A flashlight
A piece of notebook paper
Kitchen sink
Two clean large, clear glass jars with tight fitting lids

Procedure

ASK AN ADULT TO HELP YOU DO THIS EXPERI-
MENT. DO NOT USE MATCHES BY YOURSELF!

Tear the piece of notebook paper in half. Twist and
crumple the half of sheet of the paper lengthwise. Remove the lid from one jar and place this jar in a sink.
Have an adult light the crumpled paper with a lit
match. Have an adult drop the burning piece of paper
into the jar and tighten the lid on the jar. The jar should
fill with smoke when the fire goes out.

Take the flashlight, the jar of smoke, and the empty
jar into a room that you can make dark by turning off
the lights. Place the jar of smoke on a table where it will
not be disturbed. Make sure the bottom of the jar is not

hot before you set it on the table. Turn off the room lights, and turn on the flashlight. Shine the light from the flashlight through the side of the empty glass jar. Make your observations.

Shine the light from the flashlight through the side of the glass jar filled with smoke. Move the beam of light up and down the jar. Make your observations.

Repeat your observations with the jar containing the smoke every ten minutes for thirty minutes. You can turn the flashlight off and leave the room when you are not making observations.

Observations

When the room lights are on, what color is the smoke in the jar? Can you see a beam of light from the flashlight inside the empty jar? Can you see a beam of light from the flashlight inside the jar filled with smoke? What color is the smoke when the light from the flashlight passes through it? Does the beam of light change when you move the flashlight up and down the outside of the jar of smoke? Does the smoke appear to be moving?

Can you still see the flashlight beam in the jar with smoke after twenty minutes? Can you still see a beam of light in the jar with smoke after thirty minutes?

Discussion

Fuels like coal, gasoline, diesel fuel, heating oil, and wood are made mostly of chemical substances containing carbon and hydrogen. Such fuels are called hydrocarbons. Hydrocarbon fuels are burned to make energy. This energy can be used to run a car or airplane, to keep us warm in the winter or keep us cool in the summer, to make light so we can see when it is dark, to cook our food, and to make things we use everyday.

When hydrocarbon fuels are burned to make energy,

the carbon and the hydrogen in the fuel combine with oxygen in the air to make carbon dioxide gas and water vapor. Often the burning of these fuels is not complete. Not all of the carbon is converted into carbon dioxide. Some of the carbon is converted into carbon monoxide, which is a poison. Some unburned carbon particles are also made. These unburned particles of carbon are called soot. The combination of soot and the gases made during the burning of fuel is called smoke. Soot is what makes smoke visible.

In this experiment you are showing that smoke contains tiny particles. When you shine the light from the flashlight in the jar containing the smoke, you should see the beam of light. The tiny soot particles are reflecting the light from the flashlight. This reflection of light by the soot particles causes the light beam to be seen. If you look carefully, you can actually see the tiny soot particles and they may appear to be moving.

In the empty jar, there are no particles that can reflect the light from the flashlight. This is why you should not see a light beam in the empty jar.

The soot particles eventually settle to the bottom of the jar because of gravity. The larger soot particles should settle first. After thirty minutes, the air in the jar containing the smoke should appear clear. When you shine the flashlight through the jar, however, you may still see the light beam because some smaller soot particles may still be in the air in the jar. Eventually, all of the soot particles should settle to the bottom of the jar, and you should no longer be able to see a beam of light in the jar. When soot in the environment settles, it makes things dirty.

One way to reduce the amount of soot particles and carbon monoxide in the exhaust smoke from automobiles is to pass the exhaust through a catalytic converter. Catalytic converters contain precious metals such as platinum or palladium. These metals can cause unreacted carbon particles and carbon monoxide to react more completely with oxygen to form carbon dioxide and water.

Other Things to Try

Try to determine how long it takes before you can no longer see the flashlight beam in the jar that contained the smoke.

Of all the fossil fuels, natural gas burns the cleanest. Some people heat, cook, and make hot water with natural gas. Ask an adult that has a gas cooking range to show you the flame on their range. You should see a blue flame and very little smoke.

Experiment #16

Can a Charge Help Remove Dust Particles From the Air?

Materials

A balloon   A sweater

A flashlight   A dark room

A source of dust (a fabric-covered chair works well)

Procedure

Ask a friend to help you with this experiment. He or she can help create extra dust in the air for this experiment.

This experiment may not work if the air is humid or damp. It is hard to charge a balloon when the air is damp. Try to do this experiment when the air is dry. Air is usually drier in the winter than in the summer.

Go into a dark room that has a fabric-covered chair. Turn on the flashlight. Hold the flashlight so the beam of light shines across, and several inches above, the seat of the chair. Ask a friend to hit the seat cover several times with his or her hand to stir up some dust. You should be able to see dust particles in the flashlight beam.

Ask your friend to hold the flashlight. Inflate the balloon and tie it off. Charge the balloon by rubbing it in your hair or on a sweater for thirty seconds. Ask your friend to pat the seat cover several times again. Move the charged balloon near the dust particles in the beam of light. Observe what happens to the dust particles. After thirty seconds, shine the flashlight beam on the surface of the balloon. Look at the surface of the balloon.

Observations

Do the dust particles appear to jump at the charged balloon? Can you see much of the dust particles on the charged balloon? Do any of the dust particles on the surface of the balloon appear to "jump off" the charged balloon?

Discussion

A major source of particulate matter, or dust, in the air is from the burning of fossil fuels like coal in power plants and factories. Coal is a solid and is made mostly of carbon. It is the carbon in coal that burns. Coal also contains other materials, such as minerals, that do not burn.

When coal burns, most of the carbon in the coal is changed to carbon dioxide gas. However, some of the carbon remains unburned and forms soot. Soot is made of fine particles of carbon. Soot can be carried out a smokestack with air and other gases heated from the burning of the coal.

Fly ash is also produced when coal is burned. Fly ash is made of tiny solid particles of minerals found in coal. Fly ash can also be carried out a smokestack. Fly ash, soot, and gases from the burning of coal make smoke.

One way to reduce the amount of soot and fly ash escaping a smokestack is by capturing these tiny particles. This is done with electrostatic precipitators. Electrostatic precipitators are large containers that are attached near the bottom of the smokestack. Electrostatic precipitators remove particles from smoke using electricity. As the particles in the smoke move through electrostatic precipitators, they become negatively charged by the electricity. Next, these negatively

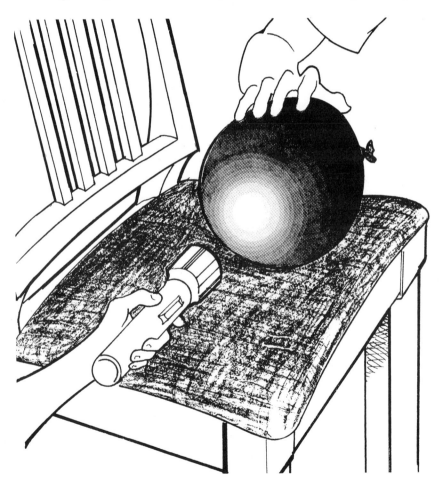

charged particles are attracted to and stick to a large surface in the precipitator that has positive charge. This happens because opposite charges attract.

In this experiment you show that dust particles can be captured with a charge. When you rub the balloon in your hair or on a sweater, the balloon becomes negatively charged. Most of the dust particles you see in the beam of light have the same number of positive and negative charges on them. They are said to be electrically neutral. When the charged balloon is brought close to the dust particles, the positive charges in the dust particles are attracted to the negative charges on the balloon. Some of the dust particles actually stick to the surface of the balloon.

Sometimes you may see dust particles that are sticking to a charged balloon appear to "jump off" the balloon. Some dust particles do this because they take some of the negative charge from the balloon surface and become negatively charged, too. They jump off the balloon because like charges repel.

Other Things to Try

Obtain some wood ashes from an adult who has a fireplace. Sprinkle some wood ashes on a piece of wax paper. Charge an inflated balloon by rubbing the balloon in your hair or on a sweater. Bring the uncharged balloon near the wood ashes. Are wood ashes attracted to the charged balloon?

Complete List of Materials Used in These Experiments

A
Air Quality Index
AM radio
apple

B
balloon
bottles, glass
bowl, plastic

C
cake pan
clear, carbonated drink in a
    plastic bottle
cotton ball

D
dark room
dirt, dark

F
fingernail polish remover
flashlight

G
glass, tall

I
ice cubes

J
jars, large
jars, tall
jars with lids

K
knife

L
lime powder

M
magnifying glass
matches
measuring cup
measuring cup, 2-cup glass
measuring spoon
milk, nonfat dry

P
pan
paper, notebook
paper plates
pen
pinwheel

R
rayon cloth
refrigerator freezer

S
sand, white
saucepan, metal
scissors
sink
source of dust
steel wool
stove
sweater

T
tape
thermometer, outdoor
toy car, battery-powered

V
vinegar

W
water

INDEX

mesosphere, 21, 26
methane, 33
molecule, 6, 51, 57
Mount Pinatubo, 73

N
neutron, 7
nitrogen, 11, 15, 82
nitrogen oxide, 16, 62, 70

O
ocean, 50
oil, 33, 50
oxygen, 11, 15, 16, 19, 82
ozone, 22, 53, 62, 68, 69
ozone hole, 54

P
particulate matter, 90
photochemical smog, 62
plankton, 51
pollution, 21, 30, 57, 73
polymer, 6
proton, 7

R
radiation, 26
radio waves, 25
rainbow, 82
rust, 15

S
sea breeze, 31
shell, 50
smoke, 57, 58, 87, 90
smog, 57, 62
solvent, 62
soot, 77, 87, 90
steel, 15

stratosphere, 21, 26
sun, 25, 82
suspended particulate
 matter, 82

T
temperature, 35, 39, 46
thermal inversion, 57
thermosphere, 21, 26
troposphere, 21, 26

U
ultraviolet radiation, 22

W
weather, 21
wind, 21, 30, 31